TOP 10 ANIMALS AT RISK

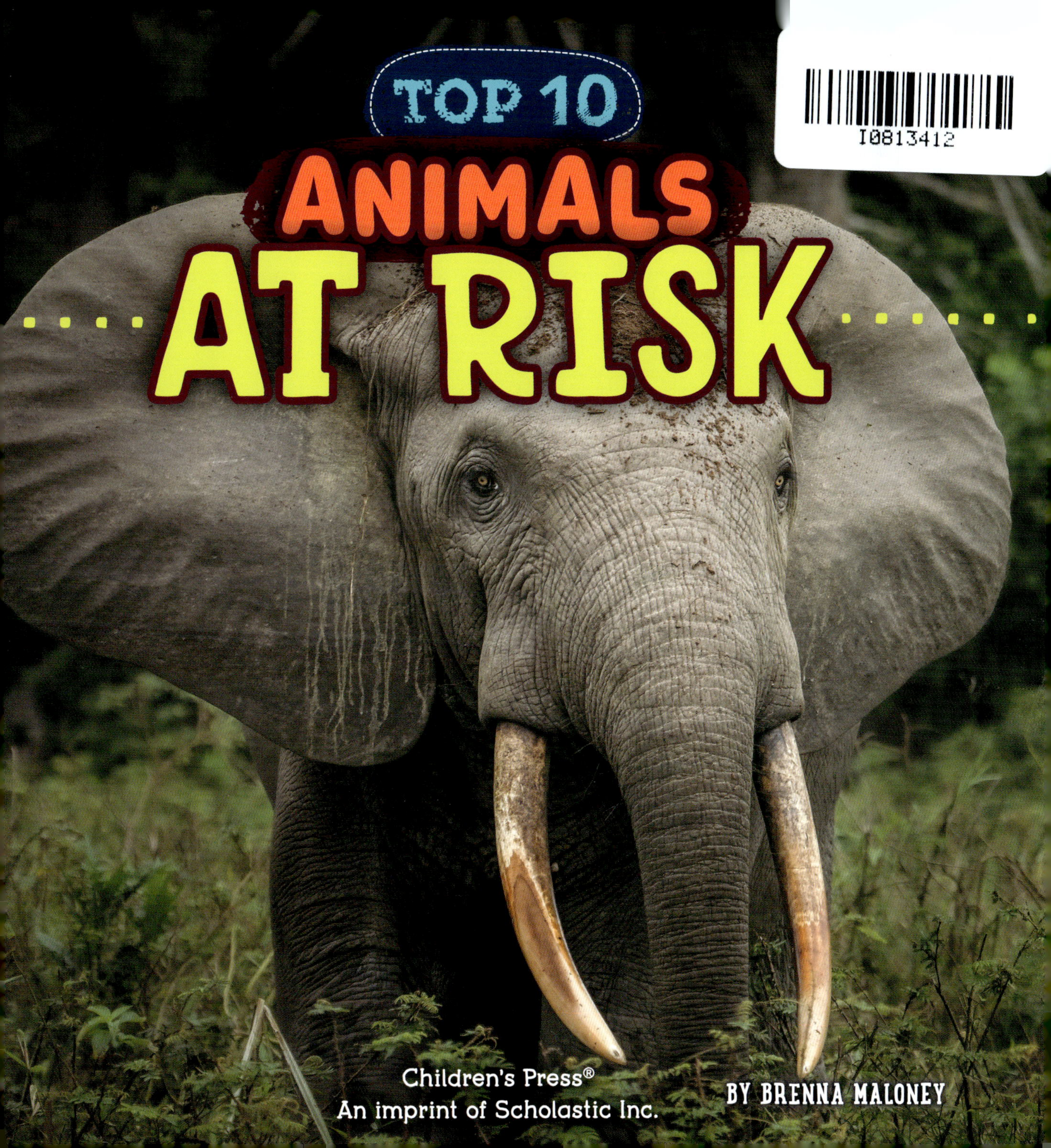

BY BRENNA MALONEY

Children's Press®
An imprint of Scholastic Inc.

A special thank-you to the Cincinnati Zoo & Botanical Garden for their expert consultation.

Library of Congress Cataloging-in-Publication Data available

ISBN 978-1-5461-7751-7 (library binding)
ISBN 978-1-5461-7752-4 (paperback)

10 9 8 7 6 5 4 3 2 26 27 28 29 30

Printed in China 62
First edition, 2026

Book design by Kay Petronio

Photos ©: back cover left, 2 left: Education Images/Universal Images Group/Getty Images; back cover right, 2 right: Gerald Kuchling; 5 (pupfish): USFWS/Olin Feuerbacher/National Park Service; 5 (leopard): Kathleen Reeder Wildlife Photography/Getty Images; 5 (turtle): Gerald Kuchling; 5 (saola): Copyright 1999 William Robichaud, Ban Vangban Village and Wildlife Conservation Society (WCS)/Saola Foundation; 5 (gorilla): Erik Pearson/Getty Images; 6 bottom: freestylephoto/Getty Images; 7: Lee Dalton/Alamy Images; 8–9: Fabian von Poser/imageBROKER/Shutterstock; 10–11: McDonald Wildlife Photography Inc./Getty Images; 10 inset: 3alexd/Getty Images; 11 right: Colin Langford/Getty Images; 12–13: Joe Austin Photography/Alamy Images; 13 right: C. DANI I. JESKE/DeAgostini/Getty Images; 14–15: David Hulse/Saola Foundation; 15 right: Copyright 1999 William Robichaud, Ban Vangban Village and Wildlife Conservation Society (WCS)/Saola Foundation; 16–17: USFWS/Olin Feuerbacher/Wikimedia; 17 right: USFWS/Olin Feuerbacher/National Park Service; 18–19: Tui De Roy/Minden Pictures; 18 inset: Ratikova/Getty Images; 19 right: Robin Bush/Getty Images; 20–21: User10095428_393/Getty Images; 21 right: ricardoreitmeyer/Getty Images; 22–23: Tobias Nowlan/Getty Images; 24–25: Marko Steffensen/Alamy Images; 25 right: Paula Olson/NOAA/Avalon/Newscom; 26 top, 27, 28–29: Gerald Kuchling; 30 top left: Education Images/Universal Images Group/Getty Images; 30 top right: Gerald Kuchling; 30 bottom left: erwinf/Getty Images; 30 bottom center: Colin Langford/Getty Images; 30 bottom right: Tobias Nowlan/Getty Images. All other photos © Shutterstock.

Who Counts?

Our "In the Wild" figures come from the International Union for Conservation of Nature (IUCN). Scientists and researchers go into the wild to gather information about the animals they see. They write down how many animals they find. The IUCN uses this information to make a list called the Red List of Threatened Species.

CONTENTS

ANIMALS IN DANGER

Did you know some animals are **endangered**? This means there are not many of them left in their natural **habitats**. And they are at risk of becoming **extinct**. Why? One reason is because their habitats are changing. Weather, natural disasters, and human activity can all harm habitats.

Each endangered animal has an important role in our world. So, people are finding ways to help them! Read on and count down from ten to one. Let's find out which animals need the most help to survive.

ANIMALS AT RISK MAP

#10 AFRICAN FOREST ELEPHANT

FACT FILE

ANIMAL GROUP: **Mammal**

AVERAGE SIZE:
As tall as a basketball hoop

DIET: **Herbivore**

HABITAT: Rainforests

IN THE WILD:
Fewer than 70,000

The number of African forest elephants is getting smaller. The rainforests where they live are being cut down. And these elephants are hunted for their tusks.

Forest elephants are important to the habitat they live in. How? Elephants eat seeds. The elephants walk around. They poop the seeds out. Trees start to grow. And new forests begin. Fewer elephants means fewer new trees.

GOOD NEWS! A group of experts in Africa is helping forest elephants survive.

AFRICAN FOREST ELEPHANT CLOSE-UP

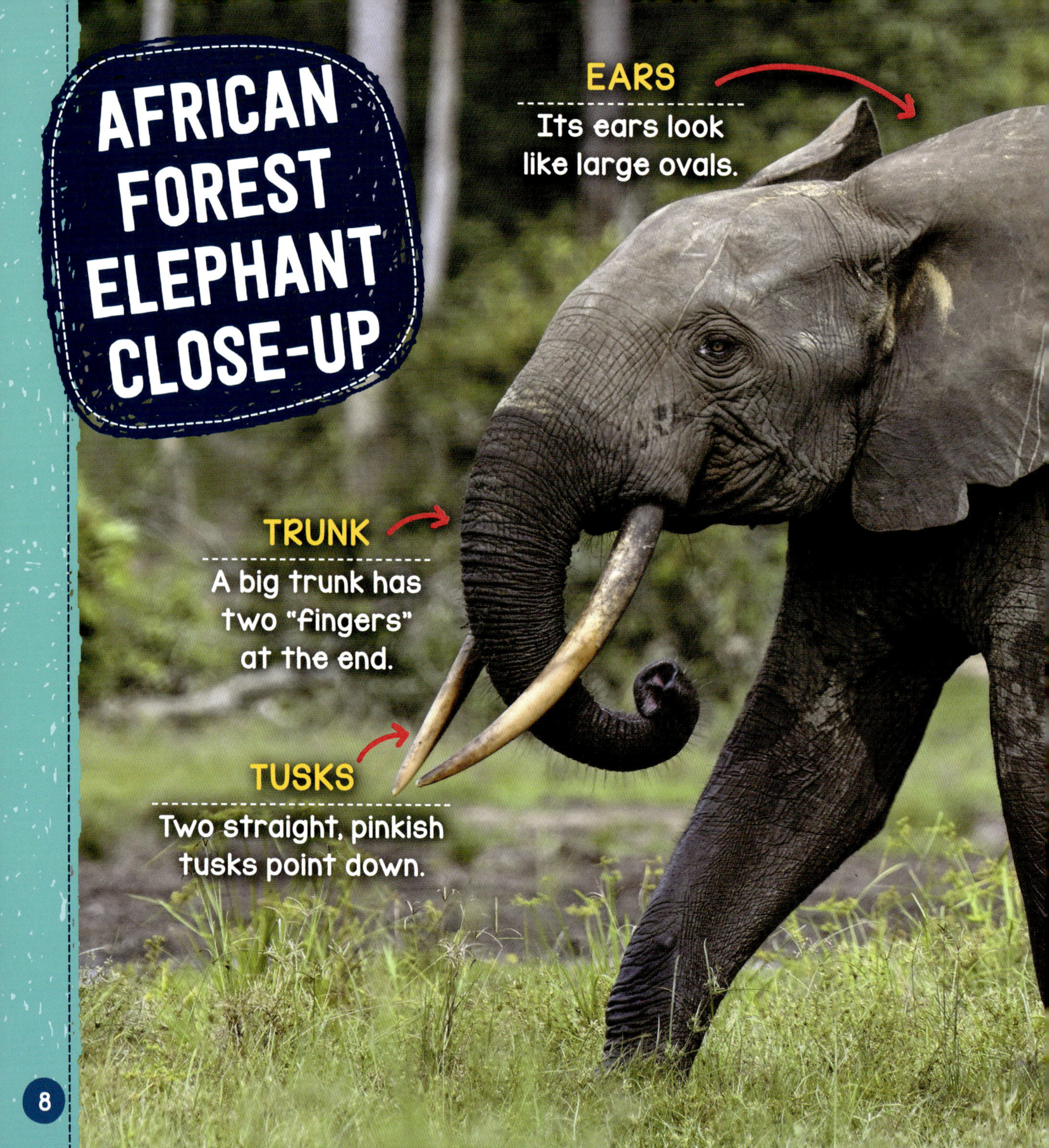

FACT

Scientists call these elephants "mega-gardeners." They help seeds grow like gardeners.

Mountain gorillas are one of the world's largest **primates**. These apes have big muscles. They have strong bodies. Gorillas eat a lot of plants. Like elephants, they poop the seeds out. New plants can grow.

Their strength also helps their habitat. They make paths in the forest as they walk. The paths let more sunlight reach the ground. The sunlight helps plants grow.

GOOD NEWS!

A park in Africa protects more than 300 mountain gorillas.

#8 GHARIAL (GEHR-ee-uhl)

FACT FILE

ANIMAL GROUP: Reptile

AVERAGE SIZE: A canoe

DIET: Carnivore

HABITAT: Rivers

IN THE WILD: 650

Gharials are closely related to crocodiles. Adults mostly eat fish. They have long, skinny noses. Their top and bottom teeth fit together like a zipper.

Gharials live in rivers. They are important because they eat big fish. That leaves smaller fish for people to catch and eat.

GOOD NEWS!

Asian countries are working together to stop gharials from disappearing.

#7 SAOLA (SAW-la)

FACT FILE

ANIMAL GROUP: Mammal

AVERAGE SIZE: A large dog

DIET: Herbivore

HABITAT: Forests

IN THE WILD: Fewer than 300

Saolas are big helpers in their habitat! The plants they eat make room for other plants to grow. Saolas were first discovered in 1992. We still don't know much about these mammals. They are rarely seen.

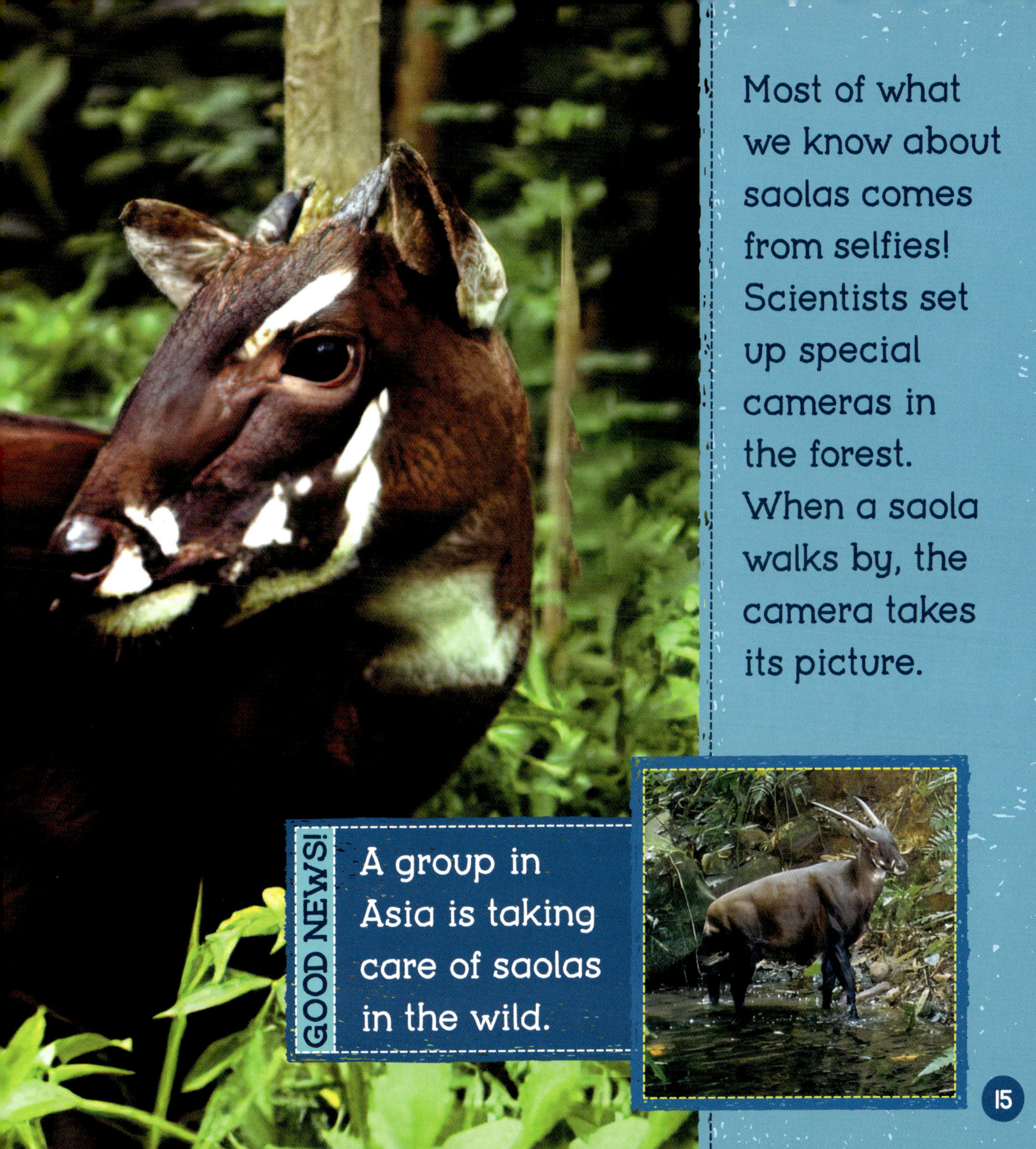

Most of what we know about saolas comes from selfies! Scientists set up special cameras in the forest. When a saola walks by, the camera takes its picture.

GOOD NEWS! A group in Asia is taking care of saolas in the wild.

#6 DEVILS HOLE PUPFISH

FACT FILE

ANIMAL GROUP: Fish

AVERAGE SIZE: A penny

DIET: **Omnivore**

HABITAT: A freshwater cave

IN THE WILD: Fewer than 200

Devils Hole pupfish can be found in only one place. They live in a water-filled cave in Nevada. The water is warm year-round. Every spring and fall, scientists dive into the cave. They count the tiny fish.

The Devils Hole pupfish was one of the first animals to be called endangered. People learned that animals like this fish need protection.

GOOD NEWS!

The number of pupfish is growing! More fish were counted in 2024 than in the past 25 years.

#5 KĀKĀPŌ (KAH-kuh-poh)

FACT FILE

ANIMAL GROUP: Bird

AVERAGE SIZE: A large loaf of bread

DIET: Herbivore

HABITAT: Forest islands

IN THE WILD: Fewer than 120

The kākāpō has been around for millions of years! This bird cannot fly because it is too heavy. It stays on the ground. It looks for food at night. This keeps it safe from **predators** in the daytime.

The kākāpō is important to its home. It eats fruit and spreads the seeds. This helps new plants grow. With fewer kākāpōs, there are fewer plants in the forest.

GOOD NEWS! A group of scientists in New Zealand is supporting kākāpōs.

#4 AMUR LEOPARD

FACT FILE

ANIMAL GROUP: Mammal

AVERAGE SIZE: A coffee table

DIET: Carnivore

HABITAT: Mountain forests

IN THE WILD: Fewer than 100

Amur leopards are at the top of the food chain. They hunt smaller animals. This helps keep the balance of animals in their habitat. It also allows plants to grow.

This is because there are fewer animals that can eat the plants. There are not many Amur leopards left in the wild. But there is good news. Their numbers are growing! This is thanks to **conservation** efforts.

GOOD NEWS!

There is protected land for Amur leopards in Asia.

#3 JAVAN RHINOCEROS

FACT FILE

ANIMAL GROUP: Mammal

AVERAGE SIZE: A small car

DIET: Herbivore

HABITAT: Tropical forests

IN THE WILD: Fewer than 20

Javan rhinos live in only one protected place on the planet. It is the island of Java in Asia. Javan rhinos help their habitat in two ways. They trample down plants as they move through the forest.

This helps control plant growth. They also love to roll in puddles. This creates natural watering holes for other animals to use.

GOOD NEWS!

People raise money to help Javan rhinos stay safe in the wild.

#2 VAQUITA
(vah-KEE-tuh)

FACT FILE

ANIMAL GROUP: Mammal

AVERAGE SIZE: A bathtub

DIET: Carnivore

HABITAT: Shallow waters

IN THE WILD: Fewer than 20

The vaquita is the world's most endangered marine mammal. This is due to illegal fishing. Little is known about this **porpoise**. It wasn't discovered until 1958.

Vaquitas are important because they help the ocean. They eat fish and squid. This helps keep a healthy balance of animals in the water.

GOOD NEWS! A group in the United States is working to save vaquitas.

#1 YANGTZE GIANT SOFTSHELL TURTLE

FACT FILE

ANIMAL GROUP: Reptile

AVERAGE SIZE: A guitar

DIET: Omnivore

HABITAT: Wetlands

IN THE WILD: 1 known

Which animal is the most endangered? It is the Yangtze giant softshell turtle. There is only one left in the wild. And a total of two left in the world.

Could there be more? Possibly! This turtle is Earth's largest freshwater turtle. It is very heavy! In the wild, it stays out of sight. It can be found in murky rivers and lakes. Scientists continue to look for more of these animals.

GOOD NEWS!

The country of China has created protected areas for this turtle.

EYES
Its eyes are near the top of its head.
HEAD
Its large head is shaped like a cone.
SNOUT
Its pig-like snout pokes out of the water for breathing.
NECK
A long neck helps the turtle snap at prey.
FEET
Wide, webbed feet make swimming faster.

YANGTZE GIANT SOFTSHELL TURTLE CLOSE-UP
SHELL
Its shell is wide, smooth, and soft.
TAIL
A short tail is hidden by its shell.
FACT
These turtles can live to be 100 years old.

SIZING THEM UP

There are many endangered animals on Earth. Each one is valuable. They remind us that nature needs to be cared for. These special animals need our help to survive. You can learn even more about endangered animals. And discover your own ways to help them!

GLOSSARY

carnivore (KAHR-nuh-vor) an animal that eats meat

conservation (kahn-sur-VAY-shuhn) the protection of valuable things, like plants and animals

endangered (en-DAYN-jurd) a plant or animal that is in danger of becoming extinct, usually because of human activity

extinct (ik-STINGKT) no longer found alive; known about only through fossils or history

habitat (HAB-i-tat) the place where a plant or animal is usually found

herbivore (HUR-buh-vor) an animal that only eats plants

mammal (MAM-uhl) a warm-blooded animal that has hair or fur and usually gives birth to live babies

omnivore (AHM-nuh-vor) an animal that eats both plants and meat

porpoise (POR-puhs) an ocean mammal with a rounded head and a short, blunt snout

predator (PRED-uh-tur) an animal that lives by hunting other animals for food

prey (pray) an animal that is hunted by another animal for food

primate (PRYE-mate) a member of the group of mammals that includes monkeys, apes, and humans

reptile (REP-tile) a cold-blooded animal that crawls across the ground or creeps on short legs; most reptiles have backbones and reproduce by laying eggs

webbed (webd) having toes that are connected by a fold of skin

INDEX

Page numbers in **bold** indicate images.

ABOUT THE AUTHOR

Brenna Maloney is the author of many books. She lives in Washington, DC, with her husband and two sons. One day, she would like to see an Amur leopard and mountain gorillas.